But Here Are Small Clear Refractions

But Here Are Small Clear Refractions

ED PAVLIĆ

First edition, 2009
ISBN 0-6153340-8-3
Library of Congress Control Number: 2009940808

Design by Megan Mangum, Words That Work
Cover photograph by Ed Pavlić
Author Photograph by Tracey Lee Williams

Published by the Chinua Achebe Center for
African Writers and Artists
Bard College
Annandale on Hudson, NY 12504
WEB: achebecenter.bard.edu
EMAIL: achebecenter@bard.edu
PHONE: (845) 758-7837

The Chinua Achebe Center for African Writers and Artists
was established in 2005 to expand the legacy of Chinua
Achebe, Charles P. Stevenson Jr. Professor Emeritus at Bard
College. Among its goals are to support a new generation
of writers and artists; to encourage literary/cultural entre-
preneurship; to introduce America to the most dynamic
and adventurous writing coming out of Africa today; to
create opportunities for African writers and literary institutions to work on joint projects with International writers
and literary institutions. To always serve the highest of
ideals and ideas.

—for Mzée and Muhammad

ACKNOWLEDGMENTS

Many many thanks to people who read this book along its way into being : Stacey C. Barnum, Michelle Chilcoat, Nathalie Handel, Terrance Hayes, Yusef Komunyakaa, Reginald McKnight, Adrienne Rich, and Craig Werner. Special thanks to Binyavanga Wainaina, Billy Kahora, Jackie Lebo and the whole crew at *Kwani?* in Nairobi. Thanks to Binyavanga Wainaina and Thomas Burke in (and to the whole of) the Chinua Achebe Center for African Writers and Artists at Bard College. Thanks to Megan Mangum for her generous sight and numerous acts of acute caring during the design process. Thanks to the Jane and Harry Wilson Center for Humanities and Arts at the University of Georgia. Thanks to Paul Goldsmith for his guidance navigating the islands. Thanks to Muhammad Kubwa for recounting his experience and for the tour of Siu and environs. Also, thanks to A. C. Hoff who seemed to suspect that this book existed, or at least that it would exist, before I did.

CONTENTS

Certainty may be instantaneous; doubt requires duration; meaning is born of the two. When we find a photograph meaningful, we are lending it a past and a future.

—John Berger, *Another Way of Telling*

You set sail at midnight. The lights of Lamu
Town—apparently the electricity's back—fade
into the distance, the glow folds in on itself,
dialects of insinuation overlap : sleep's open
door—in ki-Swahili, mlango—to awake's
narrow eye ; the soft groan and tear-seep of
music between the slats of wood and their near
cousin, water ; salt music, a dream rolled back
in its socket. The sky's bright black privacy
holds the globe between its teeth. Three thick
ropes lay dead on the dock, living threads
tingle the bottom of the boat. With sleep's ear
to the soft wood for a second, you stare at the
narrow sand-pause of a liquid slate waterway.
Eyes closed, the wood opens. You hear the
inter-costal channel reach back its thin, hairless
arm and disappear in cursive arcs that darken
from quiet to silent as they recede. They
don't. The dunes of dusk are gone. The exact
chaos of swallows that appears an hour before
sundown trades a visual algebra of borders to
the night-blind and thin-leathered calculus of
falcon-sized bats.

Above. The seven ancient doors of Shanga.
The carved mangrove has long since dissolved
into water ; mlangos seep into underground
streams and wash to the sea. Salt-bloom aloft.
Shanga's seven. Twelve doors of Barawa. The
nine of Siu. Seven of Paté. Twelve carved
mlango of Lamu. The nine and the three of
Lamu. The wa-amu, the twelve. Washenzi,
the three. Waungwana, the nine. The spindle-
whorl structure of the sky. The iron-slag
history of salt. Stone over wood. Simple math,
watu-wa. Simple. Handclaps on the beat
blink-carved in the sky. Music in salt veins
beneath the white skin of each thin eye.

Your back's on the waterlogged wood as
threads come to life and the sky swallows the
dhow. Wood more water than wood. Your ears
fish-eye the sound. Muhammad, the captain,
at the rudder. The water is in the wood. Empty
air made of black salt swings down from the
slow-motion sky. Muhammad, the mate and
cook, on the bow. With a flashlight, he marks
shallow spots, charts the channel. Mangroves
and dunes cut the wind at its knees. The top
of the sail's taut. The bottom flaps and snaps
thick claps above your nose. Muhammad in
front must have a bail of banje up there with
him. Gauge the speed of the boat by the time
between the glow in front of his chin and sweet
clouds that play over your face. Muhammad
at the rear chews khat with Usama, the guide.
You're awake when the fire-storm of stars dives
beneath the clouds. Orion on his dusty head,
boiling in a mistway of diamond milk, at the
Equator in December. The trade winds meet
the coast, explode into towers, and vanish over
the savannah to the west.

It rains constantly during the dry season, rain
into virga on its way elsewhere than down.
Otherwhere.

In a dream, you wake when the channel
ends. The dhow's caught the lunge-rhythm
of the open sea. It's sleep if your back's wet
from the sea that seeps thru ancient wood.
It's a dream if the boat's not made of wood. A
dream, brackish, thick-grained loam of water
eats away the boat and replaces it in a saline-
petrified liquefaction. The bottomless smells
swim thru the hand-hewn, gray fibre in the
bent-black beams of nightsea. It's a horizon
if you can open your mouth and drink goat
milk from a crescent moon. You're awake if it
opens an isatine throat for the sun to emerge.
Sleep breached at dawn, the ocean's an ochre
dome. Free of dunes and mangroves, dry-
season trades sweep along the waves and the
sail's full. Muhammad's off the bow. He wraps
the rope around a wooden pulley and guides
the wind's wide tail over the boat. You're asleep
if the sky swims overhead. Awake in a dorsal
roll, the rope takes and the boat leans into a
dimensional breath of space.

Mlango. Door. The intricate heft of coastal doors. Carved frames. Elephant-proof spikes. Set in Stone. The Swahili wood is a fluid pre-history. The stone's an ancient confession of power. Mlango. They all open into secrets water holds over stone. In Lamu, you're told mlango means clan, family. Which door have you come thru? The stone asks the fluid wood, the song of invisible salt. A million tons of salt blown into clouds, rivers of secrets in the air. You stare, blind, into the sky. Black salt and the privacy of tongueflesh. Mlango moja : "the same doorway."

You're wide awake when three men get off at
the tip of Paté Island. They swim with one
arm, hold their clothes up in the other, a third
pack on a rope between their upraised hands.
Usama tells Muhammad the captain that he'll
beat them to Siu and buy that cock everyone's
been talking about before they can make their
false offers to drive up the price. Backlit by
dawn in your eye, they smile at each other and
nod as they trace their gum lines with khat
and spit bits of bark into the blue thatch of
the waves. Muhammad the mate ties off the
sail and goes back to the front of the dhow.
He takes out a tiny iron grill and fills it with
charcoal. He lights another joint and steps on
a tiny bellows to feed the coals.

Chai with milk. Dried stalks lean out of the pot and drop into the coals. Seeds pop into hard bits of flame. Strips of flat bread dipped in the chai. The sun climbs thru the trees of the channel. The tide moves out. Another dhow anchored at the dock from where the dirt path to Siu begins is stuck. Plenty of water. The anchor's sunk into mangrove roots. Three young men with a handsaw call to each other as they take turns diving down to the bottom of the channel to saw the anchor loose. Muhammad the captain holds a khat twig between his fingers, dips in his bread, and shakes his head. The sun climbs along the slope of your bald skull. Your head's an eclipse. A thousand invisible fingers run along your scalp. Minutes, the length of their nails. Mombassa Jackie, the lone woman on the boat, climbs the jetty and goes behind a bush. Muhammad the mate stares at the coals and threads a thick hook onto his line.

In Siu, you learn that Fazul Muhammad lived
here after the embassy bombings in 1998. He
married a woman in Siu. His brother-in-law,
Muhammad Kubwa, greets you at the bridge
to the village. Usama says he's got a story to
tell. But first, a tour of the town and its ruins.
The ruins ring the town. Wood seeps back up
from the ground. The silent rhythm, vendetta
in the air. Ruins of two mosques bake in the
morning heat, trees have grown thru the
stones, toppled the walls, roots thicker than
your body rope the rest upright. You've seen
Roman ruins in better shape. Muhammad
dates the mosques in the mid-19th Century.
Nothing moves. The blinding speed of the
place plays your skin. You can feel the sun
taking the world apart, if you turn away and
swing your head back, you can almost see
the plants shift and vie with each other. Ten
thousand purple trumpets reel out of vines
that hold the scene in view. Five little girls
pass on their way to the gardens in search of
peppers. One of them holds a pole twice her
height. She sticks it in each patch before they
reach in with their arms.

You sit outside on the welcome bench at the center of the town. The men assemble to narrate the history of Siu. By chance, you're at the end of the bench, far from the narration. Someone hands you more chai and your skin tone on fresh samosas with spice-bouquets and goat meat in them. Body language. The men talk like men talk. To your left, a woman on her haunches in front of a dung and mud wall. She's washing dishes in three tubs. Down on haunches. Washes over the soap. Rinses in the second. Rinses in the third. Two other women, much older, sit on steps under a thatch roof with three silent children. People, all men, pass on the path. One with a donkey. One with a length of new thatch. The old women call to each man, young and old. All of them answer without a pause. Answer again as they pass. One replies in a single, unbroken ascending tone. Another in a duet of failing cadences. You haven't heard a vowel or a consonant. None of the men look at the old women.

With each phrase from the old women, the woman washing smiles. Bright streams of water run over her hands. Down her arm and off her elbow as she wipes her brow with her upper arm. She never looks up. Nods down into each sky-filled tub. None of the children speak. None of the children move. You turn. The men are pointing this way and that. You turn back and look at the alphabet of women and children. Turn. The sun's on the other side of the wall, taking apart the ruined mosques. The trees in the grove twist along, a time-lapse sovereignty of ancient snakes.

By the time you look back, there's another
woman with a new load of laundry and two
more tubs. The cadences intensify, something
narrows and quickens in their speech. At each
pause, one hum-moans up or down into the
window of speech. You understand nothing,
of course, but you feel the antiphonal rhythms
in the muscles of your face. You zero in on
harmonium wires that connect speaker and
listener in ki-Swahili, infinitely variable,
singular ; they bridge whisper's-length space
between lips and ears, they twirl thru traffic
across boulevards. The duet to your left makes
your eyes thirsty. The women pass pieces of
cloth back and forth, they've broken off from
the older women and the silent children.
Turn. The men have ceased pointing into the
distance. Caps pushed back off foreheads,
they stare at each other, then away ; their cups,
lengthening pools of silence.

The tea's gone and you're off. Later you ask Muhammad what you missed, the history recounted by the old men. "History?" His eyebrows up in amusement. "They learned where you'd come from and spent the whole time criticizing Lamu for the sorry way the people there treat their donkeys. Then, they bragged about the beautiful donkeys of Siu. Well-fed. Rested. Oiled. They said the donkeys of Lamu are more like flea-bitten dogs than donkeys."

You sit in the schoolyard under a tree. A kind
of air-borne surf at the edge of the shade
where the eleven o'clock sun heats dust and
the air rockets thru the trees. Three storks ride
the wind. They look like goats hang-gliding.
Other storks sit, hunch-shouldered and
esoteric, along the wall of the Omani-era fort.
Boys frenzy the canal. Three men at the far
edge of the yard hold a fighting cock the size of
a small ostrich. You'd been on a boat all night.
On your back in the ancient motion of fixing
points against sweet waves in the Swahili sky.
The seven and the nine. Twelve of Lamu. The
nine and the three. If the fish swims thru the
trap of points, you're asleep. If he's caught, it's
a dream. Awake is the color of the path thru
the early morning forest-miles to Siu. Awake
or not, you'd traversed the ruins and back.
The dry-season sun pours down light in silent
sheets of bright-blind hail. You're sure that if
you nod off for an instant, the sun will cleave
you like wine poured into hot ash, a tree will
mosque you in its roots.

A few years ago, Muhammad says agents of
the Kenyan government came to Siu and told
him who Fazul Muhammad was. After eating
lunch the agents told him they must arrest
his father. After accompanying his father to
Mombassa, they arrested him as well. This is
his story. There are others. Silent sovereignty
of roots over stones. Bright, deaf hail of dry-
season light. Alphabet of a riot in the canal. A
little girl's wrist and a staff in the pepper bush.
An engine of tide pulls an anchor deeper into
a tangled vein. The stories merge ; they smell
like papaya rind rubbed over rope-burn on a
palm. Muhammad speaks to us in English.
Glances thrown thru ki-Swahili to Usama.
Most of three years in prison. There are details.
"I learned, when they'd show up to transport
us, to eat well before we left. I'd say, 'you'll
have to wait, while I fix my father his meal.'"
Muhammad's story goes on and on. The
heat's turned your chin into lead. You feel a
trap door, a wooden silence—a silence that's
no emptiness—under a rug in Muhammad's
voice. The door opens into a vein traveled by
these other stories. Overnight in vans along
the road from Nairobi to Mombassa and back.
Wrist cuffed to brass rings braised into the
roof. All in all, he shuttled three years between
the simple abuses and endless mathematics of
questionings by Mosad and CIA.

You wonder how you're hearing Muhammad's
voice, crushed wide-open in the soundlessness
of the full vein, low-tide moon pulls water
from the canal, the lightning weight of root
over stone, sun and hail of boys in the channel,
deaf stream down the golden arm into the
blank stare in the wild bull's-eye of the cock off
in the shade. You decide you're only awake if
you are willing to lie and claim you don't know
you're asleep.

Muhammad's finished his story. You float face down. Drowned in a green syrup shook down from the leaves. He has a paper with dates, notes. An emptied clip of hot air, sudden diagonals in the shade, catch the corner of the white sheet. He stares at the stone holding down the notes. At once, you see how chords of air in his voice braid themselves into a visible force. Each strand of force pushed against others in the braid. You think : this is Muhammad's voice. You think : whose voice is this? This green fluid you've soaked in?

You'd never heard or seen it quite so clearly : something abruptly change and so—make no whisper of "yet" here—and so fluidly remain itself. With slack in the rope, he says he doesn't appreciate the Kenyan government's forfeiture of its sovereignty. The rope snaps tight. You figure a drop-chart for execution by a fall in the tone of a voice. The first flung aside the door, the second took the plunge. The voice floats before your eyes, the tone's gone to the bottom of a shaft, a well. You begin to sink. Descending green. You stare at its belly from below. Nothing has changed in his voice. You spin. You're in the branches of the trees. You look down at its back from above. The weight of something—peace you'd call it but it's not peace, quiet you'd call it but it's not a space—a fullness fastens to your wrists and ankles and begins to pull.

He says he doesn't know any of us except Usama : "You came here on that path, the same path Fazul Muhammad walked. He left in the night. You'll soon walk out of here in the sun. There are no hotels in Siu. When you arrived here, we had tea made by old Azir's wife. There were no prices. An open fire. There are no price tags in Siu. If one of you stays here, you'd stay in a home. If we'd like, you could stay there for weeks and leave never having been here at all and never know it. Or not. This is where you are." The stone wall of Bwana Mataka's fort in the distance behind him, he smiles down at the petals of a flower on the desk between you. "Fazul fell in love with my sister. I saw that happen." A small vein appears and ox bows its way across his temple. "I saw that happen ; that's who I am. We all saw that happen. That's who we are." Eyes closed. "Who would I be to try to stop it? Who would we be?" Open. Muhammad's left hand presses the loose fabric of his shirt to his chest: "I told them that ; we let it happen. They asked if we knew who he was? I said, 'he was a visitor, a devout teacher, a serious person, he married my sister.' Once I asked if my questioner, he was an Israeli, had a sister?

I asked how well he knew his sister's husband? He said, 'I know him well enough to know if he's a terrorist.' I asked how well he thought he knew himself. He said, 'don't get smart.'" Muhammad stares at the flower, "I'm not sure now, that one might have been an American." A motion as if he's brushing a fly out of the air with his right hand, "There were many."

You're awake if you stare into the sun and
you can't tell if it's the shadow of branches,
or a geometry of mangrove veins in the silt
of the channel. Muhammad hasn't stopped
speaking, "it appeared to me that they retained
me there for so long, really, because they just
weren't interested in what I had to say. Not at
all, and somehow they couldn't believe that.
It took them three years to know that. They
still don't know that. They'll probably be back.
Lost then as they were the first time, knowing
nothing but exactly what they came to find."
You're asleep if he stops talking and you feel
yourself let go of the branches—they might
be roots—that pattern the kind of green you'd
call a dream if you could find a place outside
of it to pretend you were awake.

In Nairobi, you'd seen Americans, red spilled
up along the veins in their necks, shake their
heads when their hotel beds weren't ready for
check-in at 11:30. The incessant eye-drone of
ipods, an invisible audio membrane covering
their eyes. Closed is closed. Phone flipped
open, they check the time in Boston. In L.A.
You thought about the silent sovereignty
of snake-roots dismantling the abandoned
mosques of Siu, the pleasure-bright streams
of water laugh down the woman's arms as
she listens to daily questions and the smiles
of serious, put-to passers-by. A parade of
characters read right to left. East to west.
"Three days without my luggage" someone
tells you while a Tusker beads, sweats into a
ring on the table. "One more, I don't know
what I'll do."

A basket hangs from the thin line of a crook in
a little girl's elbow. Toes tap. A stick probes a
thicket full of blister-red peppers. Your fingers
roll a hundred shilling note in your pocket.
You're awake if you can count the illusions as
they jump the fence into these helium-tones of
so-called American anger.

From the galactic absence of proportion in this luggage-less voice, the network of fluffed tones infecting this American idiom grows across your vision. Anger. Consumer-lingua? You see green again. You breathe what you see ; short of breath, you think "this isn't anger at all ; it's an opaque Teflon of fear. It's disillusionment. Terror." You remember ki-Swahili spread as a trade language. Lips disappear. Laughter slips across a Teflon sheet. You think : "a one-sided coin." Walking the path back from Siu to the dock, someone asked you of Muhammad, "why do you think he's not angry?" You said nothing then, mute in the wash and still searching the drop in Muhammad's tone that altered everything about his voice and left it, somehow, completely unchanged.

Now, you can see the patterns in the two greens, you map the difference : "Muhammad is angry. That's anger." The fish in the green-rooted sky swishes its tail and disappears into the sun.

It's sleep : an image hangs in front of your
face, your fingers drum its skin. You hear the
drum tone of a ripe breadfruit. It's a dream :
you say, "it's pain." You're awake if you can
see the river up ahead vanish in the sun on the
road. You're asleep at the wheel if you can see

it's no illusion. You're awake if you're standing
in the dry bed, holding the anchor.

You figure anger has serious preconditions.
You hear the braid of Muhammad's voice, the
ripened breadfruit of his tone : "no hotels,
this is what I saw. They fell in love." When
he arrived at his point about US and Israeli
suspicions of—their disbelief before and lack
of interest in—the open sovereignty of Siu,
you felt his tone drop. The rope snapped and
his voice fell into something in itself that was
not its own. Possession swallows its tail. In the
green-shaded pattern of shade, of shades inside
shades you encountered a pulse of things, of
things that aren't things.

This pulse between things inclines them one
to the other and reserves—in each—what
they'd forfeit—to each other—to possess
themselves. The music of possession which
can't be possessed. A pulse that can't be
detained ; there's a fullness that won't respond
to interrogation. Something else, an elegant
surplus that, by the fact of its being, asks its
own questions.

Sitting on that broken desk in the dust of
the schoolyard in Siu, you met it again : the
blues : a vantage from which the tragic isn't
cause for disillusionment. You can see that
from there and only from there, can anger
be itself. Like fear and joy, and like pain and
love, this anger communicates between itself
and its surroundings. At the broken desk,
you'd heard anger restored to its connection
with acuity. Without this blues, this acuity,
this rope of fullness wound—from beyond
it—in to Muhammad's tone of voice, life is
bereft of discernment and people are unable to
arrive at coherent, meaningful preconditions
for anger or for anything else. Without these
preconditions, anger—to say nothing of joy
or love and no matter the noise level—has no
volume, no fullness. Absence of these drains
silence of what fills it transforming it into
a haunted kind of emptiness. Finally, this
withering renders privacy impossible—by
sapping the singular kind of pressure private
meanings require—leaving no privacy, only an
aloneness surrounded by mirrors ; Echo's dress
rehearsals for the Pageant.

Muhammad's story—though the rhythm and tone of his voice tell another—is really an instance in such a pageant, gone to egregious lengths, arrived at Siu in its battle against itself—terror—while under the mistaken impression it's at war with an enemy. From this concocted notion of "here" emerge mad visions of (impossible) "objectives to achieve." Something smells like cassia-sweat and curry colored dirt, it sits in your ear. A live wire calls back to itself in Muhammad's voice and holds the space in "now here" open. For others, it's collapsed. From the "ever-there" made of a collapsed "now here," the Teflon-blind encircle the world with razor wire and imprison themselves on the other side of what they'll need to live. Likely, some among them imagine that they'll have to crush others to protect themselves. Points on a grid without the patterned space behind. Dimensionless space. The sound of much American conversation. The word for the surface-area of a sphere vanishes. Dimensional circumferences veer toward zero, volume explodes. Emptiness everywhere. It's real : a dreampain, realgone, fleshtorn. In the end, they'll crush the fallen grid, gasp with collapsed lungs, and suffocate themselves under their own weightless weight.

The group takes up a collection, three thousand shillings to replace his cell phone. Muhammad waves to the canoe while two men pole toward the mouth of the now-shallow canal. In the end, Mombassa Jackie bought the chicken. She paid six hundred. It makes quick for the open space at the tip of the bow. The captain's anchored beyond the mouth of the canal. The mate's rigged a sheet's worth of shade, caught and cleaned four fish. Two-dozen barracuda steaks dry in the sun like a platoon of exhausted parentheses. In the distance, four men pull a net out in the sea, swim an arc and bring it back to the beach. The air's a fresh chai and milk. Salt. You're asleep if you throw grains of sunlight over your left shoulder. You're awake if a pool of yellow oil smokes over the question that glows inside the black iron of the grill. Each blink's dust-blue script across lime burnt white on a cracked plaster wall. It's a dream if it's anything like Muhammad the mate's fried fish and, somehow, you can taste in the bone what's rubbed on the skin.

A BRIEF GLOSSARY OF TERMS

Banje : marijuana
Khat : plant of East Africa, used as stimulant
Mlango : door, clan.
Washenzi : commoner, lowly person
Waungwana : patricians, owners
Wa-amu : people of Lamu
Watu-wa : visitors, newcomers

NOTES

—"but here are small clear refractions" comes from Adrienne Rich's poem, "Trace Elements" from *A School Among the Ruins.*

— Lamu and Paté Islands are part of an Indian Ocean archipelago stretching toward Somalia along the northern coast of Kenya. This conversation took place on December 26, 2006. The United States began bombing the Kenya-Somalia border area during the first week of January, 2007. Of these attacks, on January 9, 2007, Mohamed Olad Hassan wrote the following for *Forbes Magazine:*

> *The attacks happened about 5 PM local time Monday after the terror suspects were spotted hiding on a remote island on the southern tip of Somalia, close to the Kenyan border, Somali officials said. The island and a site 155 miles north were hit.*

> *The main target was Fazul Abdullah Mohammed…Fazul, 32, joined al-Qaida in Afghanistan and trained there with Osama bin Laden, according to the transcript of an FBI interrogation of a known associate. He came to Kenya in the mid-1990s, married a local woman, became a citizen and started teaching at a religious*

*school near Lamu, just 60 miles south of
Ras Kamboni, Somalia, where one of the
airstrikes took place Monday.*

*Largely isolated, the coast north of Lamu is
predominantly Muslim and many residents
are of Arab descent. Boats from Lamu often
visit Somalia and the Persian Gulf, making
the Kenya-Somalia border area ideal for him
to escape.*

— Siu town is located in Lamu district, Coast
province in Paté Island, across the tidal
channel, which bisects the island at high
water. It lies some 25 km to the North East
of Lamu town and can be reached by boat
from Lamu, up a long mangrove lined
creek which is only navigable at high tide.
(Source: www.museums.or.ke)

A Silence That's No Emptiness...
An interview with Ed Pavlić
by A. C. Hoff

Hoff: The Kenyan writer Binyavanga Wainaina, in an essay published in *Granta,* gave some advice on how non-Africans should represent Africa. He wrote: "Never have a picture of a well-adjusted African on the cover of your book, unless that African has won the Nobel Prize. An AK-47, prominent ribs, naked breast, use these. If you must include an African, make sure you get one in Masai or Zulu or Dogun dress." How conscious were you of Wainaina's guidelines while writing "...but here are small clear refractions"?

Pavlić: Well, not at all, really. At least I hope not. Though, in fact, I wrote this series and then mailed it to him, and I said, "I think I broke every one of your rules, man. Let me know."

Hoff: There weren't any AK-47s in your work, none that I saw, and no protruding ribs, either.

Pavlić: No, no, clearly. Binyavanga's satirizing a kind of writing about Africa that you often see in journalism, in travel writing, in these kind of NGO-based liberal, sympathy-development-laced portrayals: starving, drought-ridden, war-torn, desperate images of need. For middle class, liberal readers, there's an allure associated with people in extremes. These extremes, in fact, spark a restricted part of the "fantasy-mind" (confused by some with the imagination) while comforting people in the West by erasing their own, local vocabularies for struggle and the troubling texture of their lives.

Hoff: Thank God, I'm not there?

Pavlić: Exactly. And that brand of writing—for one instance in the blizzard, the January 24, 2007, piece in *The New York Times* about a performance of Verdi with the headline "Making Music Speak for Those Without a Voice" accompanied by a wistful photo of a young Sundanese woman; the only things black pictured at the performance are the evening wear, the music stands, and the wide-open mouth of the singer who we're, I take it, to believe is delivering Verdi's voice on the young Sudanese woman's behalf—does nothing to represent the actual lives of negotiation and creativity, triumph and suffering, and the kind of tenuous balance people achieve—day by day, minute by minute—in their lives in order to live them. Of course, depictions of these nimble negotiations might be more disturbing to many western readers than images of abject suffering. One's duty to feel one way or another, for example, might not be written on a sledgehammer. As a rule, empathy is eye to eye and more difficult and dangerous than sympathy because it requires (even creates) points of identification.

Hoff: So did you feel conscious about how you would represent Africa while you were writing?

Pavlić: Well, I wasn't out to 'represent Africa'; merely to chart a hair-thin line of perception en route to an island off the coast of Kenya and back. And, the few people I mention in the poems, most notably Muhammad Kubwa, are real people about whom I know very very little. I'm conscious of that. And, you know, I wrote these pieces without really any consciousness of a reader at all. It's interesting for me, at this point, to wonder who this "you" I keep talking to in the pieces might be. In some way, I think it's a bizarre choice of pronoun. But, it's there. I was attempting to chart sensations I encountered on this voyage. I was radically out of my element. I don't speak ki-Swahili. Yet, of course, I attend things, or possibly they attend me, very intensely. I've imagined that the "you" is me and the voice is coming from various unidentified aspects of the world around me. Not quite.

Nonetheless, I was out of my element. For one thing, most Americans don't spend much time around extant, ancient patterns and cultures. Let's face it, the United States murdered its extant, ancient cultures. Quarantined the survivors… Few Americans imagine their lives in realistic relation to these patterns. It's beyond dream-catchers, etc.

So, here I was on a sailboat the precise likes of which have been sailed along the coast of Kenya, Somalia, Tanzania for a thousand years and more. I don't speak the language. But, I could appreciate its rhythms. I love instrumental music. Jazz. I also knew enough to know that I was moving in a culture which had shrugged off the influences (while retaining various aspects) of multiple empires over the centuries. Arab, Indian, Omani, Portuguese, British. The contemporary Kenyan state has a tense relationship to the cultures of the coast and the islands. And, I understood that, whether I liked it or not, a present empire has its stamp on me. I'm also aware of, am part of, I'm never truly outside of, intense cultural struggles within that empire.

Hoff: You mentioned Yusef Kumanyakaa as one of your primary influences. Do you still consider him a primary influence? What poets do you think influenced these Kenya poems?

Pavlić: With no close competition, the single most powerful 'external influence' on these poems was and is Keith Jarrett's *The Carnegie Hall Concerts* from 2005—especially movement number two on the first disc which I listened to hundreds of times in the weeks I spent drafting and re-drafting them. He plays solo piano on the album. Still, meeting Yusef in 1995 was important to me then. Knowing him has been important to me ever since. Reading his work and talking with him about all kinds of things, well, kind of helped me establish a series of rough principles to check off against in writing. I hope these pieces break some of the rules I thought I'd had. I hope they don't violate principles I say I respect. And, it seems to me in reading my recent, unpublished work, there's an impulse to image a world that we can recognize and share. I'm not sure I see much of this impulse around me in 'contemporary poetry,' and I'm not sure why. If the direction of my work is any guide, I must be responding to that in some way?

Hoff: Is it too divorced from the author?

Pavlić: It's the sense of extremity, the sense of having to go so far away from any recognizable, communicable meaning, vision. I wonder what's really pushing us in that direction? I'm not sure I fully trust the answers I'm getting (mainly here from myself).

Hoff: You talked earlier about not wanting to

say too much about your writing before you put something down on paper. Can you say more about that need?

Pavlić: I think, in conversation, we rehearse things and pattern them in a way that can become difficult afterwards to crack back open and give the actual pushing of the pen across paper the freedom to do what it needs to do. After writing, I hope, we can talk about these things, because it's a beautiful part of life, I hope. But, I find the before and after sequence of these thoughts troubling. I guess I hope our conversations can inform writing in useful ways and vice versa. At this moment, I guess I'm a bit trapped in the idea that writing fills a kind of breach between a person and the life lived by their personality. I remember being stunned at what I found after writing my way beyond the easy and uneasy borders of my personality. I think that's what a lot of the experimentation is about. The question is, what's the proportion, where's the balance? Why all the hide and seek?

Hoff: Was this your first trip to Africa?

Pavlić: No, I had lived in Nigeria in the past, but I'm not widely traveled in Africa. But going there did renew my sense of certain things. It becomes clear, well, I don't know whether it becomes clear or not, but it comes to the surface, that life in the West, and in the United States in particular, owes a lot to massive institutional power. The government and business institutions in the United States exert massive influence on our lives, ambiguous influence, influence that gives things a flow and a stream, that produces anxieties in us about whether we're a part of it or not a part of it, and that makes us perceive our positions relative to these institutions with great intensity.

In Nigeria in 1995, during a military dictatorship, most of the institutional power I encountered was overtly malignant and—thankfully—malfunctioning. In Kenya, in 2006, in December, when we arrived there, what I perceived very clearly and very quickly is that the institutions just aren't nearly as powerful, and so they don't provide anything like the services that Americans feel either are, or should be, provided. They don't claim to provide them, and very few people expect that they would, or ever could, or should provide them; so it's a drastically different relation to institutional life in general. Relative to the proportions in the United States, a tiny number of Kenyans participate in that institutional life and with a vastly different sense of expectations. A massive number of Kenyans really make things happen (namely their basic sense of themselves) without it. So, Nairobi's bus depot might have 400 buses parked in its vicinity. To an outsider the situation looks chaotic, a jumble and tumble of independent actions. There's no obvious kiosk that tells which aisle—I saw no aisles—to go to and which bus goes to where, how many people it seats and what it costs. It's kind of a swirling array of angles, gestures, arrivals and departures. Of course, there's a robust order involved and the people who are involved in it understand its coherence. It's not the kind of coherence that operates at the tick of a Swiss watch. You might not get to Kigali in 36 hours. It might take three days. But, I have the sense that it's the kind of coherence that operates if there's a watch or not, a coherence that operates even if the watch is smashed.

Hoff: Is anything translated into English?

Pavlić: English is, in fact, a good marker for all this, because everything that happens in relationship to the international world, travelers like me, happens in English. Most of the other trade, the meaningful, local trade happens in ki-Swahili as far as I could tell. And of course, English, ki-Swahili and a few dozen other languages are constantly boiling around in the everyday speech of Kenyan life. Language is a good measure and it's endless in its complexities. But, the bottom line seems to be: if you can't speak ki-Swahili, at least, the world of robust Kenyan coherence just is off limits to you. You're not sophisticated. This is a troubling position for a poet to be in. I hoped in the poems to recover a sense of that complexity while having, of course, to end-run the bottom-line rule above. I don't know if that's possible?

Hoff: In the last section of your Kenya poems, you write about meeting a Kenyan named Muhammad. You had an interesting way of describing Muhammad. You wrote, "You feel a trap door, a wooden silence, a silence that's no emptiness— under the rug in Muhammed's voice." Could you talk more about that line in your poetry, and that experience in general?

Pavlić: We visited a relatively remote town on Paté Island. Muhammed Kubwa is from this town, Siu. He told us a story about being detained by Israeli and American intelligence officials, and being questioned over a two and a half year period about his associations with Fazul Muhammad, who was married to his sister. That sentence has to do with what I heard in the tone of his voice as he recounted various things related to his detainment. I can't read that sentence, I wrote it after all. But, I was surprised, among other things, to find a voice with a rug and a trap door in it.

Many Americans made comments to me about the lack of "anger" they perceived around them in Kenya. I'm talking about the coastal islands, Nairobi struck me as an extremely angry and violent place. Several people were stunned that Muhammad Kubwa didn't seem to be angry. I recall not being too interested in the question during the time we spent listening to Muhammad Kubwa. It wasn't a question of whether or not he was angry. For me, I was interested in the tonal register of his voice and the unassuming way he related these events of terrific intensity to us. I was amazed by what I imagined to be the texture—a texture that evades American adjectives—of what I took to be his seriousness.

Hoff: The idea of unregistered injustice seems to come into play a lot in the character of Muhammed. Could you talk more about that?

Pavlić: Over the weekend a friend of mine mailed me an article from the *Washington Post* about an American interrogator's nightmares about his duties in Iraq. One of his assignments was sleep-deprivation, to deprive detainees of sleep while they were being questioned. Strangely, or not, now he's home (he thinks he's home) and *he* can't sleep at night. The story's full of horrors of abuse.

Muhammed Kubwa didn't tell us any fantastic stories of being shot with electricity, beaten with hoses, or paraded around with no clothes. He said they didn't feed him well. There could be long intervals between meals and he talked about that. His father was old and they couldn't get him a decent place to sleep, so he slept on the floor sometimes, and his father took whatever little mattress they had during the time that they were detained together. This isn't the spectacle of abuse you see in those fantastically dreary and naïve reports (because, of course, abuses like this go on in American prisons and in American police departments every day) and the infantile kind of shock they seem to provoke in many Americans. Remember, we're talking about a nation that claims not to have known that New Orleans was full of poor black people until a hurricane brought about its destruction.

I think Americans miss the point of all this. Of course, such torture is criminal and disgraceful. The necessity of having to make this point is itself shocking and disturbing. And, as we see, it is necessary to make that point. But, the cost in energy and distraction of having to belabor a question of basic barbarism does bear serious costs. It obscures crucial, less obvious but equally important realities.

Because, the point isn't simply that people are hit with hoses or tied up with electric tape, or that there are dogs sicked on people, the point isn't that that's going on. That's the spectacular and terrifying tip of an iceberg. To me, the more basic point, and so the more formidable danger, is that most of these people are in detainment for the reason Muhammad Kubwa was there: they were associated with someone in their communities, in their families. Their daily existence has been criminalized. American Indian, African American communities, Chicano neighborhoods and families know this condition very well. The very fact of their existence had been rendered "probable cause," at least. This shouldn't be news to anyone, either. It's certainly not news to me. Muhammad Kubwa's presence, however, came across to me very different from most American narratives of such situations.

Hoff: So they're guilty until proven innocent?

Pavlić: Yes, that's the issue, people detained without probable cause, etc. But, as I listened to him talk, it seemed to me that Muhammad Kubwa was serious about interesting, somewhat different things. His seriousness didn't seem dictated by the powers that held him. His perspective seemed active, alive; it wasn't reacting in the terms offered it by the powers, foreign after all, which had descended upon him. If anything, he played down his detainment, in fact. It was a criminal waste of his time, though he claimed to have met a bunch of interesting characters along the way. He said the questions he was asked were ridiculous questions. And of course, he had nothing to say, anyway.

But, the basic point was that there's a level of cultural disrespect and an insidious violence implicit in situations which are not spectacularly violent and that kind of thing is invading people's lives by the millions. It's not just the number of people detained and killed. It's the general level of disrespect sown into the world at the hands of the United States and other countries that align themselves with the United States.

Muhammad Kubwa said, in effect, "I was detained because people distrusted the way our community operates. They didn't believe we'd take in an outsider without fingerprints and lie detectors." He was defending Siu's sovereignty, their way of being open to the world. Of course, he also noted an intense, almost sacred kind of privacy as well. I'm fascinated by the relationship between these crucial, for me unresolved, aspects of life. Openness and privacy, I think we tend to think of these terms as opposed. More and more, rather than opposed, I think they're compatible and necessary to each other.

Would an American object to this suspicion? To the intrusion it invokes? Would an American have any sense of how an attack on our privacy can injure the texure of public life? And, even more, vice versa? I imagine some might object on constitutional grounds and blather about 'the rule of law.' But, haven't Americans, for instance, agreed not to think of bringing their basic self-respect, say, through an airport? Wouldn't Americans rather fantasize about safety than remain open to the world? Liquids in zip-locked baggies? What's that about? And, I think this is a personal as well as a national condition.

Consider the horrifying level of blindness and numbness in American life, how else to explain people's widespread addiction to visual media and stimulation of all kinds? So that, in the end, the level of abuse that Muhammad Kubwa takes so seriously doesn't even register as abuse among the American people. And that's my point, the level of cultural disrespect doesn't register on Americans. Why? I can only imagine that it's because we're already used to this kind of abuse. Functional American cultural selves (and the private selves which exist in such an interesting tension with cultural life) have been largely erased. They've been willfully evacuated. 'Dislocated' used to be an injury, now it seems as if it's a badge of sophistication, mobility and success. But, then again, two generations ago, 'consumption' was the commonly used name of a terrible disease. Today it's supposed to be the basic index of economic vitality. Consider the violent lack of seriousness of so much, so called "post-modern" culture. *Clerks*. The built-in, self-deprecating irony that lacerates a suburban consciousness, slicing it away from any attempt at a full presence in the world, prevents eye to eye contact. Devotion, commitment and whole spectrums of human experience have been rendered off limits. From this vantage, seriousness itself must seem a romantic concoction; extreme sports invite an endless series of desperate acts at the surface (snow, wave, concrete tube, cliff, river) of experience. Would-be workers and lovers have become headlong tourists of their own lives and the lives of others near and far. Consumer vipers have invaded seemingly every cultural endeavor. Crafts and trades which once made coherent working people's relationship to each other (and to pain) have been brutally displaced. I wonder what forces, exactly, have guided people's widespread consent in these transactions? Coercion and the 'whiteness of the will'?

The zip-locked ease of this world is lethal to a committed consciousness, the basic difficulties have been erased and replaced by so-called difficulties—careers—accessed via batteries of entrance examinations—themselves culturally coded and off-limits to most.

Far from abuse, I imagine many, many Americans regard this kind of shedding of basic difficulties (and the tin badges of dislocation which have replaced them) as a marker of success, even privilege. It frightens me to imagine large numbers of people convinced that they can live life in this kind of condition, a condition well beyond arm's length from the basic intensities of human life. A gated community, if only a point of pilgrimage in their brains. I imagine such people must be almost chronically angry. Jumpy. Edgy. Many are medicated. Muhammad Kubwa didn't display this kind of shallow, manic intensity I recognize around me in the United States. People wondered, "Why isn't he angry?" In the end, I concluded that Muhammad Kubwa is angry. I imagined that that was anger. And the pageants (private, personal, political) of American anger people were expecting to find have more to do with disillusionment than they have to do with anything that should be called anger.

Hoff: In that last section of the poems, you wrote about these American tourists who were making a scene at their hotel in Nairobi because they were upset about the bad service they were getting. Why did you include those tourists in the last section of your poems?

Pavlić: The image appeared. I'd observed this. But, the image appeared in the poem, and from it, I could see people so unsettled in the world that the tiniest inconvenience can become drastic in its effect on the personality. And that image sat in great contrast to my experience listening to and talking with Muhammad Kubwa. I'd wondered, what's that about? Finally, it seemed to me that, for some people, when confronted with inconvenience or pain or trouble, they feel taken outside of who they think they are. That's what I think a lot of the anger and tension is about. The way some people think of themselves doesn't include these experiences. So when these experiences come to the door, as they always do, a great unsettling takes place. On the other hand, if your conception of yourself somehow allows for these kinds of things, experience, then the effect would be different. And, be clear, I'm not talking about the "stiff upper lip" or a steady, ironic shoulder to hide one's chin behind. I'm talking about a sense of self that can take in and absorb the facts of life. It seems to me that a person who can absorb his experience will be able, in some way, to discern the difference between his life and the spectacle of evasion, success and so-called privilege that threatens so many Americans' sense of themselves.

This is what I imagine. Listening to Muhammed Kubwa talk, this is what I heard. I imagined a dimension of openness balanced against an intact culture of privacy. The result was that I imagined the lives around him wound into the tone and texture of his voice even in English. And so, if he wasn't talking, if he was silent, there was a fullness: "a silence that's no emptiness." And I wondered what happens if silence is still full? What's it full of? And what happens when silence becomes empty? I wondered about that. What happens to a public culture when there's no fluent privacy? When people have willingly evacuated themselves, torched the villages in their psyches and buried the remains? What's there when we're not talking? Who are we when we're not following some pursuit or goal? Strictly speaking, this isn't a question of Eastern philosophy. I'm no ethnographer. I'm not a sociologist. I'm an American poet, this is what struck me. The poems angle in on things that appeared to me and these are the questions I'm left with at this moment.

AUTHOR'S BIO

Ed Pavlić's recent books are *Winners Have Yet to be Announced: A Song for Donny Hathaway* (UGA P, 2008) and *Labors Lost Left Unfinished* (UPNE, 2006). His other books are *Paraph of Bone & Other Kinds of Blue* (Copper Canyon P, 2001) and *Crossroads Modernism* (U Minn P, 2002). His prizes include the Darwin Turner Award from *African American Review, The American Poetry Review* / Honickman First Book Prize, and the Author of the Year Award from The Georgia Writers Association. He has had fellowships at the Vermont Studio Center, The Bread Loaf Writers Conference, and The MacDowell Colony. He teaches at the University of Georgia and lives with Stacey, Milan, Sunčana, Mzée and I Am Pozzo in Athens, Georgia.

PRAISE FOR *BUT HERE ARE SMALL CLEAR REFRACTIONS*

This book is not quite prose, not really a travel book. We move through this space, with photographs, in real boat-rowing, person-interviewing, feet-walking time, in poetic and metaphysical space, the words create their own human country, and allow us to inhabit Pavlić's *question*. The world he makes begs such a question, one of those giant dangerous worlds poets and writers sometimes forget it is our job to make.

—Binyavanga Wainaina
    Director, The Chinua Achebe Center
    for African Writers and Artists

With a poet-musician's attunement to sound and silence Ed Pavlić enters the sovereign domain of Siu, a village on the remote island of Paté off the Kenyan coast, where world events (Somalia, CIA) have penetrated, echoed and receded. We learn much from Pavlić's eye and ear—acutely vibrating with social and political undercurrents. The poet as listener, camera as mind in respectful encounter with places and privacies. No clichés, no colonizing claims, no ego-indulgence. Here, depth-perception and beauty of language resist classification. This is a remarkable work, not a "travel book" but one that should travel far.

—Adrienne Rich

A world of crystal-clear reflections lives in this collection of Ed Pavlić's prose poems and photos; *But Here are Small Clear Refractions* challenges the reader long after it has been closed. And, yes, one keeps returning to these pages because the images refuse to let us go. The natural moments of magical realism transport us to a landscape primarily shaped through deep feeling, and we don't wish to exit this rough beauty. The interview at the end becomes a girder that supports the weight of shared feelings. Ed Pavlić's wonderful collection creates a bridge between cultures and voices that we can trust.

 —Yusef Komunyakaa

Ed Pavlić's poems are rituals for awareness that contribute deep music to the human condition. These insightful pieces are lyrically and visually engaging, unraveling silent beats that unite rather than divide us. A stunning contribution to international literature.

 —Nathalie Handal